© 2012 Hana Beneš, all rights reserved

http://dreamlifesecret.com

No part of this book may be reproduced, stored in a retrieval system, or transmitted by any means without the written permission of the author. The material in this book is based on data compiled by Vitalogy Research.

ISBN: 978-1470007379

> "There are only two ways to live your life.
> One is as though nothing is a miracle.
> The other is as though everything is a miracle."
>
> — Albert Einstein, physicist

"(The book) is refreshingly different. (Hana) comes at this from such a common sense, direct and simple angle that I find myself actually hurrying to turn the page in some sections… maybe it's because I agree with much that she has to say."

— Marilyn Gomes, Vancouver, BC, Canada

"It changed my life – with no effort and no conscious thought on my part I experienced a transformation so gentle, so profound and so liberating that words escape me."

— Mark Grenier, Welland, Ontario, Canada

Table of Contents

Preface   *1*

Cats Know Better   *5*

The Cart Before the Horse   *11*

Miracles   *21*

Where is the Bug?   *27*

Framed   *35*

The Show Called Your Life   *45*

The Stage, the Roles, the Actions   *51*

A House of a Thousand Mirrors   *57*

The End - or the Beginning?   *65*

About the Author   *73*

Preface

Have you ever looked back and marveled about all the mistakes you've made during the years? Have you ever wished that you were able to wind back the clock and have a chance to live your life over?

Have you ever wondered, "What's wrong with me"? "What's wrong with other people?" "What's wrong with the whole world?"

Most of us do at some point in our lives – and often for good reason.

The human race has made mind-blowing scientific progress during the past centuries. We were able to cross the threshold of outer space, to uncover riches in the depths of Earth and its oceans, and to produce weapons that could destroy it all.

We're inundated with 24/7 news, mostly bad. Causing us to live in a perpetual state of apprehension, afraid to cross a parking lot at night, frightened what may happen to our children on the way to school or even in church.

Why, somebody as safe as a grandma offering milk and cookies could turn into a kidnapper. A student in the middle of a busy mall may be an undercover terrorist... So we worry, stress, and strain. That's what we were taught to do since we started to crawl.

And by thinking about problems that may never happen, by rehashing each trial and tribulation with anybody willing to listen, we keep ourselves in an ill-fated stress response: stress causes chemical changes in our bodies, such as increased blood pressure, heartbeat, and stomach acids.

ಐಖ

That's how I lived for most of my life. Busy and stressed. I had two great children, a good husband, and I still managed to build a number of businesses. I seemed to have everything a person could wish for – and most of the time, I was more unhappy than anybody could imagine...

Those who didn't know me well would never have guessed how unhappy I was. I looked cheerful and friendly. I had a positive attitude - or at least I thought so. I smiled a lot, no matter how I felt. That was part of my lifelong training.

I tried to be everything to everybody and rated my success by other people's measuring sticks. People may have seen me as ambitious and successful but I never felt that way. On the contrary. To say that my life wasn't working would have been an enormous understatement.

And I knew a lot, as we all do. I was sure I had all the right answers but there was always a nagging feeling that something may be missing in my life.

Something was. I was. Me, myself. I had no idea who I really was and what I had going for me, as most of us don't. And being a rebel at heart, I eventually tore down almost everything that I had built.

ಸಂಡ

Then, easily and gradually, I turned it all around. I learned that after all the possible and impossible secrets and laws that have been revealed, there still remained one simple and unpretentious "secret".

One simple step that changes everything. It is like flipping a light-switch in a dark room. The darkness disappears and everything in the room looks and feels differently, although the room is the same.

What will this simple "flip of the switch" do for you?

- You will restore and re-create loving and caring relationships with your parents, children, partners, and other people around you, but first and foremost, with YOURSELF.

- You will be able to reclaim the vitality and love that you have deserved all along.

- You will be able to do what needs to be done with a sense of joy and ease.

- You will start understanding other people – why they act as they do. And, you would know how to effectively deal with it all.

ℰℬ

Read the book and do the Mini Medi-Actions at the end of the chapters.

You don't have to believe a word I say. If it works for you you'll know it. It's always better to take everything with a grain of salt and a sprinkle of common sense.

Try on the ideas I am presenting, as you would try a new pair of shoes. Do they fit? Good. If not, put them back on the shelf.

"One's first step in wisdom is to question everything – and one's last is to come to terms with everything."

- Georg C. Lichtenberg, scientist and satirist

Chapter One

Cats Know Better

When was the last time you breathlessly watched the magnificent streaks of sunbeams through the clouds? How long has it been since you took the time to enjoy the chirping of the birds and enjoyed the fresh morning air?

What about purple-tinted sunsets reflected in a pond? Too busy to notice, aren't we? – At least most of the time.

Too strained and tired after the day's work - and there's the six o'clock news, dinner, and dishes. Parking on the sofa with a remote in the palm is preferable to going for a walk. Late night movies with microwaved popcorn or maybe a hockey game and a few bottles of beer would do just fine.

Let's face it: the beauty of nature doesn't fit our lifestyle anymore. At least not for many and not often.

Why is that?

ଊଓ

Cats know better. They know how to fully relax. They don't anticipate possible problems. They handle struggle when it comes.

And soon as it is over, they shake off the tension, lick their wounds and go back to hassle-free observation of flies on the windowsill. They don't cry over spilled milk. They lap it up. Maybe we should take a few copycat lessons...

Some people don't like cats because cats just do what they want. Unlike dogs, and unlike humans as well.

We disregard what we desire and do what we think we have to. Most people waste their days in relationships that don't work, on jobs they cannot stand but are afraid to lose, earning just enough money to buy the bare essentials, whatever they might be.

Is this really the life we were meant to live?

ಜಂಡ

What about you? Have you read books, played countless tapes, CDs and DVDs, attended myriad workshops and seminars?

And while it was all interesting and enlightening, while you heard many tips and pieces of advice (some very good, many extraordinary), how much of it do you still retain?

How long did the sense of being motivated, energized, and maybe even inspired last? Likely, not long at all.

Do you, too, at times feel that you may have missed something; that your dream life may have turned to a nightmare?"

Not everybody desires large estates and fast cars. Most of us want love, happiness, health and peace of mind. We want to look and feel good, to be surrounded with people we love, and to be able to do what we want, when we want. Why don't we?

The explanation is simple. Our body-mind system was designed for the harsh conditions of a faraway past.

In the grass, in the trees, behind the rocks – danger was everywhere. The hunter never knew if he'd bring some meat for dinner or if he, himself, would become dinner to the hunted beast.

Times have changed. While we safely hunt for food on supermarket shelves and freezers, our bodies and their basic physical responses stayed largely the same. Except for the brain. It has almost tripled in size, giving us wonderful new tools such as imagination.

There is so much power in imagination. No matter

where we are or what we are doing, we can mentally transport ourselves to where we want to go: to faraway places, the past, the future, anywhere, any time. But do we use that power wisely?

> "Imagination is more important than knowledge. Knowledge is limited. Imagination encircles the world."
>
> - Albert Einstein, physicist

We can imagine being, doing, and having whatever we want. We get an immediate physical response to whatever we imagine, be it a threat or a treat.

When we imagine good things, we start our days with a smile. But more often than not, we imagine what may go wrong: The traffic jam on the way to work, the deadlines we won't be able to meet, all the problems we might have to handle – and we start our days with a frown on our face, a knot in our stomach, and tight, stiff shoulders.

Cats don't. They don't imagine problems. They deal with each moment as it arises. Who would you say is more content?

A Mini Medi-Actions

Close you eyes, lift your palms up, deeply exhale and wiggle your fingers. That seemingly trivial motion relaxes shoulder muscles and relieves stress. Keep on deep exhaling and moving your fingers for about 20 seconds and you'll feel your whole body unwinding.

Repeat anytime when feeling tense.

Hana Beneš

Chapter Two

The Cart Before the Horse

Do you remember when you were growing up? The experience of newness, the bounce in every step, the eagerness to learn and discover how things work. You can see it in the sparkling eyes of a child.

Recall your old dreams. What did you want to be? A charming princess, wonder mom, private detective, alluring movie star? Superhero, race car driver, firefighter, pilot? Did you want to write the best books, direct heroic movies, save the world?

What happened? How did your life turn out? Do you live your dreams, or, are you starting your days wishing you didn't have to drag your feet out of bed? Most people do the latter – and there are many good reasons for it.

Everywhere we look, we see overwhelming problems, many virtually impossible to solve. From personal eccentricities, family and community difficulties, to serious global predicaments. Disappointingly, the majority of them have been created by us, by the human race.

However, we have the perfect excuse for it all. "We are not perfect."

Or are we? Would God (under any name) throw a monkey wrench into His last – and as far as we are concerned - most important project and make humans less perfect than a snowflake?

"Man was made at the end of the week's work when God was tired."

- Mark Twain, writer

Good shot, Mr. Twain. Nevertheless, what kind of all-powerful Almighty would tire after such a trivial task as creating a few galaxies, some light, some water, and covering the earth with flora and fauna?

Could it be possible that in this universe, where every seed, every leaf, every butterfly, and every spider is formed with painstaking perfection and loving precision, that one – and only one species – would be excluded from the equation?

Hardly so. Not the design of Homo sapiens! But, yet, our perceptions and assumptions are flawed.

It wouldn't be the first time in history we got things wrong...

※

Leading mainframe computer companies declared that there would be no market for personal computers.

The Swiss watch industry flatly rejected the prototype of a digital watch, invented by a Swiss citizen.

Just a few centuries ago, the Church was resolute that the Earth "was flat" with the sun and moon spinning around it.

The list goes on and on.

※

So where do we err, when it comes to our own perfection?

Consider that our bodies have two distinctively different modes of operation: **harmony mode** for day-to-day living, and **discord mode** for moments of acute and actual danger.

We are always in a perfect relationship to the mode that our bodies are operating in.

When in **harmony mode**, we feel safe, serene, happy, full of compassion and love. We are in harmony not only with the whole world, but even with the next-door neighbor who plays his music a little too loud.

We focus on what feels right and magnify all what's good in and around us. We support our partners, children, and friends in what they choose and what's important for them.

Many people try to reach ***harmony mode*** by isolating themselves in monasteries or living on roots and berries in mountain caves. That's a tough road to go, but does it work?

Separation from the human clan doesn't make things any easier: our natural drives follow us wherever we go. Also, suppressing feelings that we consider "undesirable" doesn't help. Suppressed feelings simmer until they pop like overheated popcorn.

If you've ever been in love or held a newborn baby in your arms, you know the ***harmony mode*** – or at least a trace of it.

A case in point: When in love, your skin glows, your eyes sparkle, and you float instead of walking. The lifted toilet seat doesn't matter; neither do your partner's little quirks. Dirty socks under the bed don't mean anything – and the unfortunate speeding ticket? So what?

That mode is easily triggered by anything pleasant: a peaceful sunrise over the lake, a sight of an awe-inspiring mountain or even by having a few good laughs with a friend.

God didn't make a mistake. We did. We put the cart before the horse, when it comes to how we experience the world.

We consider the *discord mode* normal, when it never has been our primary mode. It's meant to be used only when we are in danger, and spend the majority of our time in *harmony mode*.

We have created environments that propel us into the discord mode, and think of the harmony we feel in quiet moments or in nature as a refreshing exception to real life. Too bad, since that's the way we were meant to live. The mode of harmony is embedded in each and every cell of our body, ready to be used anytime.

And this is the promised secret: In spite of the worldwide evidence to the contrary, we were born good. Homo sapiens were created as perfect as a snowflake as well as the rest of the world.

We are gentle beings, generous, helpful, compassionate and loving. That's how we were born – in *harmony mode*.

Only after being painfully trained to live defensively, we became stuck in *discord mode*, turning into domineering, scheming, manipulative and vindictive creatures.

Yet, switching back to *harmony mode* is as easy as falling in love – or if that were not viable, as easy as switching from our daily complaints into daily appreciation. The wavelengths of love and appreciation are very similar.

Anytime you appreciate something (anything), you instantly swing to the divine frequency of *harmony mode*.

Begin right now by actively looking for things to appreciate: first and foremost about yourself, then about the dearest people in your life, as well as situations you find yourself in.

What do you appreciate most?

ಌಃ

The second operational mode, *discord mode*, is a part of our protective defense system. It is set off by some form of discord in our environment, by some sense of real or imagined danger. Instantly, our body-mind system turns fully alert to nothing else but the possible threat.

When in *discord mode* and on the defensive, we magnify problems by focusing on and noticing only "what's wrong." What's wrong with us, with our partners, with the whole planet.

We flaunt judgments and create crisis, brood over what must, mustn't, should or shouldn't be done, struggle with conflicts and at the same time resent any advice.

We also try to mold our partners, children, and the world at large to our own brand of righteousness.

ೲ

The change from one mode to another is swift and spontaneous. We don't even think about it. It simply happens.

You will notice *discord mode* when looking at a cat that, relaxing on the sofa spotted a strange dog in a doorway.

The cat would instantly forget the flies on the windowsill and either arch its back and bare its teeth, ready to fight, or it will become "all legs," ready to run – and if the foe seemed stronger and faster, the cat would "shrink" enough to hide in the small slit behind the sofa.

Our responses are similar.

ഏ⃝ଓ

Imagine you are walking through a park, fully enjoying colorful sun rays streaming through the trees, admiring budding spring flowers and happily mulling over a promising dinner date. Suddenly, you hear ferocious barking and see a strange looking dog darting towards you.

Would you still notice the sun rays?

Absolutely not. The beauty of the rays and thoughts of a pleasant dinner will be banished by your mind. All you would look for is a stick large enough to help, a tree you could climb or a safe spot to hide.

ഏ⃝ଓ

A Mini Medi-Actions

Every morning, as soon as you wake up and put your feet on the ground, stretch every part of your body and start the day by appreciating the fact that you are still here and that the game is not over, yet.

Hana Beneš

Chapter Three

We are hooked on knowledge. Sure, we know a lot but there is more that we don't know, don't understand and never will. And that's fine – we don't need to know everything about computers to be able to use them.

"All I know is that I know nothing."

- Socrates, Greek philosopher

We are dedicated to science, yet our scientists, who are able to calculate the precise course of countless planets, have no proven idea where the planets originated. They are familiar with all body parts and functions but have no clear-cut notion where people fade to after shedding their physical bodies.

If knowledge were as powerful as we like to make it, why aren't we all rich and happy? Why aren't we all well and healthy? Why aren't we all fit and slim?

Blinded by what we think we know, we fail to see

the daily miracles that surround us.

After all, we live on a partly chilled fireball that spins a lot and moves around the sun. What's holding it in place? What's holding us in place? Gravity, sure – but where did the gravity come from and what hidden power made it work the way it does?

As a matter of fact, every drop of water is mystifying, transforming itself from a dainty snowflake into a rainbow of colors, then into a sparkling ice crystal... until it puts on its disappearing act and evaporates into thin air.

Each apple seed contains the blueprint of a full-blown tree. An apple tree. No pears included. Every duck's egg contains the blueprint of a duck.

And each newborn baby is a miracle. Why then do we live convinced that we are not good enough?

ΩCR

You may not recall it, but at the very beginning, you didn't do badly, not badly at all. Within nine months, you had – with no formal knowledge - developed from one tiny cell into a full-blown human baby. What kind of invisible organizing life source was there at work?

During your first year, you doubled your size and re-doubled many of your abilities. You were a miracle in the making.

As a toddler, you had self-esteem; you knew what you wanted and how to get it. You also had a voice - and what a voice! - and were not afraid to use it. Until your well-meaning elders began to train you otherwise.

༺༻

You have been taught many rules, theories, laws, as well as lots of tips and secrets. Some became imprinted after frequent repetition, mostly through interactions with parents, caregivers, siblings and peers.

Some values were affected by movies, books, news stories; even fairy tales and commercials may have played a large part in your programming.

You learned how inadequate you are, how much you need to improve and how much more you need to learn.

"The first problem for all of us, men and women, is not to learn, but to unlearn"

- Gloria Steinem, writer

A few mouse-clicks in GOOGLE search illustrate how widespread the subject of our need for improvement is:

- 108 000 000 results for Self Help
- 33 000 000 results for Self Development
- 20 800 000 results for Self Esteem
- 28 200 000 results for Self Improvement

So many complex and complicated theories and strategies…

෨෬

I prefer to use a simple, easy to understand computer analogy instead.

Although the body-mind system is far more sophisticated than any computer so far invented, there certainly are some similarities: New computers come equipped with hardware and some pre-set programs.

So do we.

Our bodies perform the function of hardware. The mind is a collection of "bio-software" that we were set up with, and what a collection it is!

෨෬

You – as everybody else – started your life as a dwarf in the land of giants. Everybody around was bigger and stronger. You needed to be taken care of, to be fed, to be loved. You needed attention – and you knew how to get it. You learned fast.

ℬℭ

Babies are like a sponge. From tone of voice, a frown or a smile, they soak in "who is who" and "what is what" and imprint it into their script.

They grasp what their family considers "good", what's deemed "bad" and they either accept or challenge it. In next to no time any toddler knows the best way to get that forbidden cookie before dinner – and more.

What was the "right way to live" within your family conventions? What "programs" did you use to cope and to get what you want? Did you need to throw a temper tantrum to have your way? Was it necessary to cheat, lie, and pretend? By the age of two you had it all figured out.

You activated programs that worked. Just as with computers, so with babies: some of the programs had "bugs."

A Mini Medi-Actions

Think about miracles, about the courage of a tiny dandelion growing in a crack in cement.

We take for granted that we know the world around us, but there is so much we are unaware of.

There is true magic in the air. Radio waves, cell phone signals, wireless Internet networks, television frequencies, all that you can't see or hear without technology.

But that's not all. The air supplies our lungs with oxygen, with the smell of cinnamon buns and lilacs on the kitchen table...

Can you think about more miracles around you? Make a list – there is magic even in writing things down. Don't hold back, the longer the list, the better.

Chapter Four

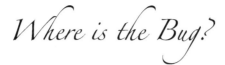

One of the mind's assets, designed for our convenience, is that when we hear, see, or do something often enough, the data gets locked in the cell memory.

Once we have mastered the task, we don't have to re-learn how to walk, ride a bike or drive a car. It becomes natural. Likewise, when we repeatedly hear certain statements, our response to them becomes automatic.

ಸಿಂಡ

You – as every other baby - were born a miracle. However, by the age of two you were convinced that you were a bad little girl or boy and that you had to "try" (and try hard) to behave and be good.

What were your unpardonable sins at these times? Did you throw the spinach they tried to force-feed you on the floor? Did you finger-paint kitchen walls with crayons or perhaps with mustard and ketchup? Did you stomp your feet when you didn't get your jellybeans?

༄༅

Your parents tried to raise you well. You, as a parent, try (or will try) to raise your children well. Unfortunately, babies do not come with how-to manuals and our parental efforts are often lacking.

And that's where the bug is: In those infamous lessons that we received between the age of zero and two:

> "Don't be a sissy."
> "You must always be the best."
> "You can't do anything right."
> "Eat all what's on your plate – or else!"

༄༅

Long before the age of six, children think that they know who they are, what's "right" and what's "wrong", what they like and what they don't and worst of all, what are they good at and what they are not. What a ridiculous assumption!

During major life events such as starting school, falling in love, getting a first job, youngsters start making new decisions. But, all those decisions become piled on top of the old and faulty root programming.

Programming they are not even aware of, just as a fish is not aware of water until a wave throws it on the beach. The same root programming that planted "bugs" into their system, molded their self-esteem and their wellbeing, shaped their attitude to other people and to what it means to be successful.

That old programming (stronger than most of the new decisions) will become the foundation for all future experiences. It will control and shape the rest of their lives – as long as they stay stuck in the *discord mode*.

ಬಿಓ

Who is to blame?

- You? NO. It wasn't your fault. As a baby, you didn't know anything about "programming" your mind. You did the only thing you could.

- Your parents? NO. It wasn't their fault, either. When they grew up, they were in the same shoes as you were. They didn't know any better.

- Society? NO. It only echoes the faulty programming of its members.

- Nobody is to blame, not even God. Let it go. It's just the way it is.

Nevertheless, that kind of programming is based on and restricted by history - by past experiences, just as computers are limited by the programs they contain.

Browsing the Internet is a different cup of tea. There we find access to new, different, and nearly unlimited information.

The brainwaves of **harmony mode** give us the ability to browse a "divine net" where we have access to the unlimited wisdom of the universe. When we are relaxed and letting our minds wonder, any questions we ask are answered and solutions to the most pressing problems present themselves as from thin air.

✂︎

There are anecdotes about famous scientists and inventors that support the dramatic benefits of relaxation.

Isaac Newton (physicist, mathematician, and astronomer) was inspired to formulate his gravitation theory when relaxing in the garden. One version of the story says that he sat under an apple tree and a falling apple hit his head, showing him the power of gravity. But would have had this epiphany if he hadn't been resting under the tree?

Archimedes (ancient mathematician and physicist) resolved his problem (determining whether silver was added to king Hiero's gold crown) while relaxing in a public bath. The legend says that, excited about his discovery, he had forgotten to dress, and shouting "Eureka", ran home naked.

Thomas Edison (one of the most acknowledged inventors of all times), when unable to find an answer would – with his eyes closed and a pebble in his hand - settle down in a rocking chair. When the pebble fell from his hand, he usually had his solution.

ಸಃಐ

The human mind is an unparalleled, complex, and remarkably powerful apparatus. It was designed to fully support your wellbeing and safety. Although it doesn't seem so, it is on your side.

"The energy of the mind is the essence of life"

- Aristotle, ancient Greek philosopher and scientist

Your mind is fine. The glitch is in the data programmed in the first twenty-four months of the tiny tot – YOU.

Contrary to popular belief, you, too, are fine and you don't need to be "improved" and/or "patched up". You actually are much better and more capable than anybody ever allowed you to believe.

Take on a new quest: discovering who you really are. You are bigger than the data in your mind and you do have the power to manage your body-mind system. Realizing that is the first step in regaining the control of your life.

What about your song? Do you even remember what you used to dream of before you were instructed that dreaming is childish and useless? Before you were ordered to pay attention to what's important, like working hard and doing what you are told.

If you were able to rewind the clock and start over, would you work harder, would you worry, complain, and stress more or would you enjoy every precious moment?

"Most men lead lives of quiet desperation and go to the grave with the song still in them."

- Henry David Thoreau, author and philosopher

A Mini Medi-Actions

What did you, as a child, hear so many times that it became "locked" in your system? Become a silent observer of your distant past.

Make a note of everything that comes to your mind. Don't judge it, don't argue with it, just look it over. Is it true or nothing more than farce?

Hana Beneš

Chapter Five

After knowing that your mind is fine, that it was designed to support your wellbeing and safety, and that you too are fine - much better and more capable than anybody ever allowed you to believe - there is something that needs to be added:

It is impossible not to notice that in spite of all medical discoveries during past centuries, we still quite don't understand why we act the way we do. Everywhere we turn, there is suffering, fighting, distress, and despair.

According to GOOGLE search, there are

- 66,800,000 results for ANXIETY

- 66,600,000 results for DEPRESSION

- 11,400,000 results for MENTAL DISORDERS

- 8,490,000 results for MENTAL ABUSE

Some of the data is valid. Some, taken out of the context, might be misleading and some issues may easily be deceptive.

When I was fifteen, I spent an hour in a mental hospital. It was one of the longest hours in my life. I was visiting a person I loved almost as my mother. She went through precarious insulin therapy, electric shock treatments, and was heavily overmedicated. Even today I shiver, remembering her bloated face and unfocused eyes.

There was only one thought in my head: this is not right. Then and there I had decided that I would find out what's wrong with the human mind. I had no idea that I had set myself up for an impossible quest. After all, at that time I was only fifteen.

During the following years I have looked everywhere and anywhere. I have studied everything that came to my attention.

At first, it seemed like a puzzle of a million pieces that didn't seem to fit. But eventually, the last piece of the puzzle fell in place – and the answer was exquisitely simple. So simple that even I, myself, found it hard to believe.

"When the solution is simple, God is answering."

- Albert Einstein, physicist

Amazingly, when I was fifteen, I had set out to discover what's wrong with the mind. Forty years later, I found what's right with it.

ೋಬ

How mysterious is the mind? Let's have a look and take away some of its mystery...

Around 400 BC, Aristotle (ancient Greek philosopher and scientist) clarified three functions of human mind:

1. FRAMES (of reference)
2. FEELINGS and
3. FORMS

ೋಬ

FRAMES stand for our thought patterns, concepts, and accumulated knowledge. They calculate and deal with what is right and what is wrong, as well as what is "good" and what is "bad".

To survive, we need to be right.

> *As a child, Herb (one of our workshop participants) tried to separate two play-fighting dogs and one of them bit him. His "frame" says that getting close to dogs is BAD and dangerous.*
>
> *Dianne (another participant) grew up in the country. There were always two or more dogs around the house. Her frame of reference on dogs? They are GOOD - protective, playful, intelligent.*

❧☙

FEELINGS represent our moods, desires, likes and dislikes.

They serve us by screening what we like and what we don't, what we love and what we can't stand. Liking and loving generate a JOYFUL LIFE.

> *Because of his experiences, Herb doesn't like dogs. Even now, as an adult, he is uneasy around them.*
>
> *Dianne, on the other hand, loves dogs. Cocky, her Labradoodle, follows her wherever she goes.*

❧☙

FORMS may be diverse. Some are visible and measurable (physical manifestation, movements), others vibrational and barely noticeable.

They bring out our natural bias and impulses, activate physical and mental responses, and trigger predictable actions and reactions.

> *When Herb sees an approaching dog, he stiffens with sore expectations. Dogs, sensing his dread and dislike, react grumpily, thus supporting Herbert's negative opinion of all canines.*

> *Dianne gently talks to any dog, and the same dog that grumbles at Herb is most likely to wag its tail at Dianne... again supporting her belief that dogs are friendly animals.*

Are these responses natural? No.

They were learned, but because of repetition they became involuntary and unnoticed. Neither Herb nor Dianne would be aware that their reactions to dogs come as pre-programmed mental packages.

There in fact is an apparatus that activates or inhibits what we are and are not aware of. It's called RAS (reticular activating system).

Have you ever lived close to a highway or an airport? Do you remember how disturbing the noise was during the first few days? After a week, you didn't even notice it.

That is one of the functions of the RAS: to choose what does or doesn't represent danger and what we do or do not need to perceive.

FRAMES (our thought patterns), FEELINGS, and FORMS (physical expressions) work like three sides of a triangle. When you change one side, the other two instantly change as well.

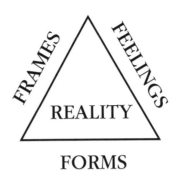

FORMS

The space between the sides of the 3-F triangle shows up as your immediate reality.

When you are afraid, your mind-frame is tangled with fearful thoughts and packed with fearful feelings. There are obvious physical signs: a knot in your stomach, sweaty palms, shifty eyes… Then there are other, less obvious signals but even dogs can pick them up.

When you are angry, your frame is crammed with angry thoughts and stuffed with angry feelings. There are instant physical effects such as a tensed jaw, shoulders, and fists, plus increased blood pressure. Blood rushing to your head would make you "see red" and no matter what happens, you'll find it irritating.

When depressed, the frame is wrapped by negative thoughts and is packed with unhappy feelings. Physical responses include slumped shoulders, tightness in the chest, head or other aches and difficulty to perform even the easiest of tasks. And again, no matter what's around you, you will see it as depressing.

When you are happy, the frame is brimming with pleasant thoughts and your heart is full of warm and fuzzy feelings. And the physical response? A switch to the heavenly frequency of **harmony mode**.

> "Nobody really cares if you're miserable, so you might as well be happy."
>
> - Cynthia Nelms, author

Did you know that a simple change from frowning to grinning affects more than fifty muscles? In less than twenty seconds, your smile relaxes your shoulders, eliminates stress, and at the same time modifies your heartbeat and blood pressure.

ഌഇ

The source of our problems is in the framework. While our thought patterns, concepts, and accumulated knowledge are passive, the frames act as molds that trigger and shape our feelings (the active ingredients of our make up).

They could be compared to a gelatin mold, shaping the actual gelatin. And, the interaction between the thoughts and feelings brings on an appropriate physical response and action.

Herb's "dog-frame", based on a single but traumatic experience with one dog may be incorrect (not all dogs are dangerous) but it is very real to him. During the years of seeing dogs' response to him, he accumulated all the evidence he'll ever need.

It is amazing how many ridiculous frames we accumulate and lock in during childhood. Never to be reconsidered. They become our personal truth.

A Mini Medi-Actions

Start focusing on what makes you feel good. Feeling good will be automatically followed by warm thoughts and pleasant physical sensations.

You have a large range to choose from. What is it, specifically, that makes YOU feel good? A pleasant memory? Looking at a picture you like? Feeling a salty breeze in your hair and wiggling your toes in the sand?

If you are serious about turning your life around, jot it all down.

Hana Beneš

Chapter Six

The Show Called Your Life

You've heard it before: You are the director, the playwright, and the star of your life-show. You choose your co-stars and assign supportive roles; you structure the plot.

If you can't believe it, I don't blame you. For a long time I wouldn't have believed it, either. Would we – in our right mind – create a life full of grief, misery, and pain? What happened to joy, out-of-this-world relationships, natural wellbeing and happily-ever-after?

"Life is but a show."

- George Bernard Shaw, playwright

True enough, but there are some differences.

We didn't set our "stage". We were born into it - into the whole family setup with many irrational rules and beliefs. The view from our crib displayed most of "our world" for way too long – and by the time our crib was exchanged for a bed, we knew the whole setup by heart.

Without looking back, we have built our lives around our family framework, no matter how unworkable. Our minds became "framed" by hurtful incidents from an early age.

൮◌ൣ

Let's face it. You were small. It wasn't easy to stand up for yourself. Some people scolded you, others laughed at you, and often, you were hurt.

Do you have to search for all that happened to you in order to heal the old wounds? Not really.

If you did, you would endlessly drag your feet with little results. Your mind is an outstanding search engine. It always finds what you are looking for. In this case it would be more and more misery.

Digging up old wounds would perpetually keep you in pain. Without exception, we always get "more and more" of what we focus on.

൮◌ൣ

Within the sphere of *discord mode*, we use just a miniscule part of our mental and sensory abilities. We grow up "framed" – and the context of those frames influences every situation, on every level of our lives.

They do need to be reopened and examined but opening them in *discord mode* is painful and not effective.

Harmony mode totally shifts your perspective. Its peaceful state affects your every perception (intuition included). You become one; not only with an irritating co-worker, but even with that all-powerful force that moves the galaxies.

When observing the whole spectrum of every incident with deep-seeded compassion (towards ourselves and others), unlocking the faulty frames is effortless. We become able to let go of the past and present pain and enjoy all the love and beauty around us.

Until then, old frames influence every situation, on every level of our lives. To feel well, we do need to reframe our lives.

ಬಂಡ

As a child, I had concluded that I was ugly. Obviously. My baby brother was the cute one. So I grew up as "ugly, but smart".

How do you think I reacted when somebody said: "You are a beautiful girl"? Did I believe it? No. My mental response would have been something like "Sure, sure" or "What does she want?"

However, when somebody casually commented that I seemed to be tired, I was crushed: "I must look ghastly..."

Years later when seeing my daughter – pretty, elegant, intelligent and looking so much like me - I got the inkling that maybe, all things considered, I wasn't that ugly. Looking through my old pictures was an eye-opener. What I saw was an attractive woman.

Too bad that I didn't spot it earlier.

ೞΩ

Were you fortunate enough to frame yourself as "beautiful"? In that case, you wouldn't worry if somebody mentioned how terrible you look.

You might consider the possibility that the other person may be blind or spiteful, you might go and check your make-up, you might admit that you feel worn out - but would that statement shake you up or change the inner perception of your personal beauty? No way.

Since I was the "smart one", I never had a problem when somebody said, "You are stupid." Yet, I know many people who had accepted a frame labeling them as "stupid" - and who would consider "That was smart" as a stroke of luck.

"I am not lovable" - that was another one of my favorites. Do you think that I have ever really heard anybody who

said, "I love you"? Can you guess how many times I have dismissed it with "If she/he only knew"?

❧☙

Relating to the world from a frame called "I-am-a-failure" doesn't let in any complements on a job well done. All successes are treated as exceptions. "It was a fluke. For once, I got lucky. No big deal."

On the other hand, when things go wrong the response is immediate: "I knew it, I knew it, I knew it."

With an "I-am-a-success" framework in place, even a major failure is greeted without trauma. "You win some, you lose some. Next..."

Noticing the frames that we are viewing our lives from makes all the difference. Once we are able to see the frames that give our lives their context, we have a chance to keep doing what we're doing, or to choose another way of seeing the world.

A Mini Medi-Actions

While reading, come up with any of your personal frames that hold you back. Write them down.

Look at them for a moment. Where did they come from? Are those really your frames or did somebody else implant them into your thoughts?

Most importantly: consider a new perspective that would provide an empowering frame to live from. Write that down as well.

Chapter Seven

The Stage, the Roles, the Actions

The "family stage" gives us our "roots" and also a limited choice of the roles we may play. It is quite remarkable how many hurtful roles we are willing to take on - and we usually keep on playing them for the rest of our lives.

Without really being aware of why, we choose our starring roles. We grow up either as "nice and good" boys and girls or we become labeled as "rebellious".

The role we take leads to a specific range of actions. As good and nice, we opt for "good deeds", while rebelling would give us the right to aggravate others.

❧☙

As a kid, I was the proverbial "good girl". I always remembered to say "please" and "thank you", usually did as I was told and didn't answer back, at least not too often. For most of the time, I was quiet, sensible, and "smart."

Eventually, I switched to "rebelling". I had no idea that rebelling is the other side of the same coin. Mistaking it with independence, I didn't know that I was still acting and reacting within my family framework.

❧☙

Roles dictate what type of people we will relate to. They define how the "derelicts" look and how the "leaders" act, they identify whom we should learn from, whom to sneer at, and whom to ignore.

At an early age, we also pick up clues from those around us and create imaginary models for ideal mothers, fathers, daughters, sons; we form opinions about police officers, kings, clowns - even the government and public servants.

We have been fooled by storybooks and we have swallowed hook, line, and sinker all of the stories about sleeping beauties and about kisses that turn frogs into princes. A noble idea, I am sure, but I have yet to see it work.

Although I have met men who at the beginning of the ball, looked and acted like princes. A few kisses later, they turned into thick-skinned frogs.

The roles also direct our actions. Yet, we expect our co-stars (especially our partners) to act inconsistently with their roles. We try to believe that they will "change" if we only loved them enough. It doesn't work that way. Roles are quite rigid and they control actions.

Drinkers will reach for a drink, slackers will find pleasure in lazing, spenders will spend freely, workaholics will work long hours... and they will not change unless THEY want to.

ഇന്ദ്ര

Our actions are powered by the roles that we have accepted and those roles direct our responses. Unless we change the role, changing our actions is ineffective.

As long as they are stuck in their old roles, smokers who decide to quit have to use a lot of "willpower" to control the craving, so do drinkers who want to stop drinking. Unless they let go of the old role and the label they've accepted and assign themselves a new role, nothing changes. A "person who chooses a healthy, happy life" would have much better chance to achieve success.

Although that is difficult when we try to do this in **discord mode**. Only in the powerful frequencies of the **harmony mode**, is it a natural and effortless process.

ഇന്ദ്ര

What about you? Are your actions bringing you the results you want? Are you satisfied with the roles you have chosen — or are you ready for a change?

There is an even more compelling step than switching roles: letting go of your family's framework and setting a new stage: your own.

Why keep on playing in Junior High performances when you can star in a Broadway show? You can create a set of frames that reflect your personal values. New frames that permit you to design new roles for yourself, and with them, new actions.

ଓଓ

It's time to choose between surviving in **discord mode**, where you would keep on struggling through problems and dis-ease, or rising to **harmony mode**, where you would share your passion, compassion, and joy.

The choice is yours. Just remember: Life is a stage production and the show called Your Life is not a mere rehearsal, even if now and then we do get a second chance.

A Mini Medi-Actions

Close your eyes, exhale deeply to clear the tension and relax. Then ask yourself: If you could have anything you wanted, what would it be?

Write your answers down and leave the paper where you will be reminded of it at least once a day.

There is power in wanting, power in asking, and power in writing. If you want to add even more power, find pictures of what you want and make a collage, or start a "wanted" file on your computer.

Chapter Eight

A House of a Thousand Mirrors

In an old Japanese fable, a happy dog waddled into the House of Thousand Mirrors and saw a thousand happy dogs, joyfully wagging their tails. "What a groovy place, I must come back often", barked the happy doggy.

Then a growling pooch barged into the same Mirror House and immediately saw a thousand viciously growling pooches. Swearing not to ever return to that menacing spot, the second dog quickly ran away.

Have you ever noticed that when you walk down the street smiling, the whole street seems to be smiling back at you? When you frown, most everybody you meet follows your lead and frowns at you as well.

A smile that comes from the heart, from the core of your very being, a smile that not only shapes your mouth but also adds a sparkle to your eyes… that's the smile that makes all the difference – and believe it or not, our entire planet acts as the proverbial House of Thousands Mirrors.

ಣಐ

If you had the choice, what would your world reflect back to you: your frowns or your smiles? How would you live if you knew that you have the power to choose?

You do have that power. To test it, lightly cross your hands over your heart and smile. You can smile for no reason, you may bring up an old amusing memory, look at a picture you like or think about a moment that made you happy. It doesn't matter.

In about twenty seconds you will feel the difference in your body. Your breathing will change and your shoulder muscles will loosen up.

Tightness around your shoulders is the first and most obvious sign of being stressed.

Your breathing will change (automatically), every muscle in your whole body will relax – and within the twenty seconds, you'll feel much better and brighter than before.

That's just one of the 1001 possible switches to **harmony mode**.

ೋಲ

We think a lot. Usually the same thoughts day after day. There is a lot of confusion about our thoughts. Some are not considered "proper" and even the "proper" ones could prove dubious.

"Thinking is what a great many people think they are doing when they are merely rearranging their prejudices."

- William James, psychologist and philosopher

Let's say "love your neighbor as yourself." Who is kidding whom? Most people are not their own best friends but their own "best enemies." No neighbor deserves the same love and treatment that the majority of us give ourselves.

The other thing we've often heard since we started to crawl is "don't be selfish." Does it mean that we should be selfless?

How can we be selfless? Everything we are, do, and have centers around ourselves, even if we prefer not to admit it.

> *Don't misunderstand: I like to do things for people and I love to empower them. But, the reason for it is totally selfish, as it should be: it makes me feel good when I do something that makes a difference in another person's life.*

ഌ෬

When it comes to our feelings, we were taught that some are unacceptable. It may be better now, but when I grew up, girls were expected to never get angry; boys were not permitted to be afraid - what nonsense!

So-called negative feelings (sadness, frustration, anger, even rage) give us valuable survival tools when we are in jeopardy.

- Anger provides extra strength and stamina.
- Sadness is a healing process for grief.
- All other feelings we label "upsetting" are crucial components of **discord mode**.

Unfortunately, we consider **discord mode** the only way to live.

When it comes to interactions between thoughts and feelings, there is another interesting point that people are generally not aware of: We were convinced that we cannot do what we want and that it is our duty to do things that we find insufferable.

There may be times when we cannot avoid the conflict between what we want and what we have to do but these should be exceptions, not the rule. These conflicts have a far-reaching impact on our health and wellbeing. We are at our best when we do what we love and love what we do.

※

The point is splendidly displayed in one of the tarot cards, the Chariot. It shows a picture of a coachman and a coach pulled by two differently colored horses (red and blue in most decks).

The coachman represents YOU. The coach depicts your actions and their consequences. The blue horse stands for your thoughts, the red one for feelings. As you have surely noticed, one horse is pulling to the left, the other to the right.

What is the message?

When your thoughts and feelings pull in opposite directions, your experiences, actions, and results will be chaotic and your life-journey will turn into a "bumpy ride".

There is another piece of wisdom hidden in that picture. Notice that the coachman who represents you is the one - or at least should be the one – who is in control.

You are not your body and you are not your mind. You are the intangible energy source, sometimes called spirit, other times soul, observer or witness, who is holding the reins.

You are not your body and you are not your mind. You are the invisible source of unlimited possibilities.

"You are not a human being having a spiritual experience. You are a spiritual being having a human experience."

- Dr. Wayne Dyer, author, lecturer, and philosopher

A Mini Medi-Actions

Instead of reacting to your thoughts and feelings, observe them as if they were clouds reflected in a bubbly creek.

Don't judge them, just observe as they come, flow, and slip away - come, flow, and slip away - come, flow, and slip away.

Learn to be a silent mind-observer.

Chapter Nine

The End - or the Beginning?

We humans are quite extraordinary. The difference we have made in science, health-care, communications, transportation and space travel is mind-boggling.

However, the progress didn't come without side effects: personal, interpersonal and global crises threatening not only our safety but also the safety of the whole Earth.

Most of the actions we are taking don't seem to be working. How many decades have we been – with negligible results - "fighting" poverty, cancer and all other autoimmune illnesses as well as abuse, terrorism and crimes?

> **"We cannot solve our problems with the same thinking we used when we created them."**
>
> - Albert Einstein, physicist

It may be that we can't – as the saying goes - see the forest for the trees.

Do you wonder why? Most of our thinking patterns and emotional responses are locked in the limiting frequencies of **discord mode**.

There is nothing wrong with **discord mode**, on the contrary. Each so-called negative emotion is an excellent tool for our protection (when needed) and our survival in dire emergencies. And it is based on many different forms of fear.

Fear is an important tool as well. It's a warning that something in our surroundings is "wrong" and threatening. We were born equipped with a few basic types of fear, namely fear of falling, fear of a loud noise.

Only later on we were "trained" to be afraid of other things. Afraid to speak, to touch, to feel... Afraid what people would think about us.

ಸಿಂಡ

*How preposterous! You are a caring and generous person. (We all are. So loving, so bighearted, so kind. It comes to us naturally when in **harmony mode**.) Still, sometimes, when you feel hurt or angry, you may act like a complete fool. (We all do when in **discord mode**.)*

People can see you either way – or anywhere in between. However, what traits they choose to see says a lot about them and not much about you.

ඊඏ

Thanks to the unfortunate "training", most of us have lost our voice. You probably know that public speaking ranks as fear number one, fear of dying comes second.

Do we really have to be afraid of dying? We have no idea where we came from and where will we go after death. Before a butterfly spreads its wings, the caterpillar has to die.

**"You don't have a soul.
You are a Soul. You have a body."**

- C. S. Lewis, novelist and literary critic

Is it so hard to consider the possibility that we, in death, also leave the cocoons of our bodies behind and fly toward the light?

It may seem like a simple play with words but there is a powerful difference between having a soul and being one.

ඊඏ

You ARE a Soul. You were born to live in harmony with yourself, others, nature, and the whole astonishing universe. You are a vital part of its makeup. You matter. You are here not to merely survive but to create.

Harmony mode *is (and always have been) your home base. That's where you started your life. You got disconnected, but returning to it is easy.*

There are a 1001 ways how but the easiest shortcut to a life full of impact and happiness is a simple smile. The smile that connects your head with your heart. Frequent smiling (and even better: laughing) will add years to your life.

ℰɔ⟨ℛ

In ***discord mode***, all perceptions that are not needed to overcome the pending or imaginary danger are stamped out. With an attacker behind a bush, our judgments are based on one factor and one factor only: our safety.

In moments of danger, our thoughts, feelings, and actions become coordinated by the hypothalamus, the primitive (some would say "animal") part of the brain. Its energy fields are underscored by anger, irritation, apprehension, annoyance, anxiety, and worries.

That's why scientific guesstimates suggest that we are using only two to maybe ten percent of our brainpower. The reason? Living with fear, in *discord mode*.

Switching to *harmony mode* truly is like flipping a light-switch in a dark room. With a soft and easy touch the darkness disappears and everything in the room looks and feels differently.

> **Harmony mode** *gives you access to full power of your exquisite brain – and more. It opens the door to "creating." Co-creating with the invisible source of life (God, if you will, under any name).*
>
> *It also gives you an access to a "divine" search engine. You will receive divine answers to whatever you ask. Just make sure that you ask pertinent questions. "Why me?" wouldn't do. As in Google, a careless question would bring vague results. The answer to "why me?" may be "why not?"*
>
> *How would you live, what would you do if you were able to use not two to ten, but twenty, forty or maybe close to hundred percent of the powers of your brilliant brain?*
>
> *These powers are and always have been yours and they are waiting for you in **harmony mode**.*

When I was young, I wanted to change the world. It didn't budge. Today, I know that the world is fine the way it is. However, by changing myself, I was able to change everything around me.

"When the power of love overcomes the love of power, the world will know peace."

- Jimi Hendrix, guitarist, composer, and singer

The majority of people serve their life sentences in the **discord mode**. *When we reverse the trend and most of us will start living in the life-giving frequency of* **harmony mode**, *the world will become a safe and loving place.*

A Mini Medi-Actions

*During next week (and rest of your life), make switching to **harmony mode** your focal project. Smile and laugh as much as you can. Focus on what's beautiful around you. Center your spotlight on feeling good.*

When feeling sad or angry, gently cross your hands over your heart and deeply exhale "love." You may choose "appreciation," "healing," "ease," or whatever you prefer.

(Don't worry about inhaling, the air will return automatically.)

*Switching to **harmony mode** is easy. It is our natural mode. Our early rigorous training, however, keeps pulling us out of its peaceful and refreshing mode. To stay there we have to practice and practice and practice...*

Yet, staying there will give a new and profound foundation to every aspect of your life. Open your heart to miracles.

Hana Beneš

About the Author

Hana Beneš is a life-long entrepreneur, but her greatest passion is learning about the workings of the mind and how it is affected by other elements and factors.

As the founder of Vitalogy Research, she created and facilitated a string of life-changing workshops, such as A Taste of Freedom, Life Begins Now, and Wellness Revolution.

At present, Hana is preparing more workshops, as well as completing her second book: "Everything is Love" is about creating a new context for deeply loving relationships.